Guy Ganachaud

Wonderful Loire-Atlantique

Photographs by Hervé Boulé
Translated by Angela Moyon

EDITIONS OUEST-FRANCE

R. Erdre north of Nantes.

Front cover : *La Baule.*

Back cover *: Saint-Nazaire Bridge.*

2

Fishing at the mouth of the R. Loire.

FOREWORD

With the word "Atlantic" in its name, this département is filled with the tang of the sea - but mind the oil! And in its skies, there are fleeing clusters of gulls. The word "Loire", too, has watery connotations, and indeed everything seems to be in perpetual movement here, either arriving or leaving. And not only for the summer holidays. As to the mild climate, it fills the air with the rich scents of many different plants.

The fairly rugged coastline of Loire-Atlantique resembles the outline of a gigantic plane tree leaf; the vein-waterways would be the Loire and certain tributaries such as the Erdre and Sèvre Nantaise. And then there are the two cracks, doubtless caused by the west wind - the Brière Marshes and Grand-Lieu Lake. Nevertheless the region is well-anchored, by Nantes and the towns round about, Saint-Nazaire, Ancenis, Clisson, Châteaubriant, Guérande. It lies like a huge leaf, covering 695,640 hectares.

Setting aside imagination and looking at the area from the more limited viewpoint of officialdom, the département has 4 subdivisions, 56 districts, and 221 towns and villages. At the last census, it had a population of more than one million, Nantes alone accounting for 247,227 of its inhabitants.

Now the capital of the "Loire Region" with Vendée, Maine-et-Loire, Mayenne, and Sarthe, Nantes once also shared with Rennes the role of capital of the province, duchy and kingdom of Brittany.

This is important for anybody seeking to understand the personality of the local people. And it is a characteristic that is illustrated by the wealth of tales and legends, the attraction for castles in the air and real action, the tranquillity and vivacity, and a taste for the Baroque combined

3

The banks of the R. Sèvre in Clisson.

Haute-Goulaine Castle.

with a love of fantasy. Like the menhir jutting up above the pastures, the past is always present. Despite all that modern civilisation has to give, Loire-Atlantique has not, or not yet, been hammered out to fit the dull uniformity of standardisation in everyday life or in things spiritual. This is confirmed by poets such as René-Guy Cadiou,

"Wrap me in forests, it's a wonderful feeling…"

The aim of this book, then, is to make this ambivalence clearer, with the assistance of photographs by Hervé Boulé, a person who is also highly sensitive to all that is unusual at a time when a general requirement for speed seems to be wearing down attention to detail.

The French of inland areas have only really known this part of Western France for two hundred years or less. With the rise of the Romantic movement, many a writer set off along the roads of Armorica in general and this département in particular, when it was known as "Loire-Inférieure". Among them was our neighbour from Noirmoutier, Edouard Richer but the visitors also included Honoré de Balzac, Gustave Flaubert, Maxime de Camp, and Emile Souvestre. And they were followed by countless other writers and artists !

From the observations of the first of these, it is somewhat surprising to learn that, in those days, Saint-Nazaire had only just over one hundred houses, that the beach at La Baule was totally deserted, and that Pornichet consisted of nothing more than a few cottages on the shores of a canal. As for the people described by Emile Souvestre, they have become well-known characters over the years.

Even today, though, you can still dream, even underneath an electricity pylon. Because living creatures and inanimate objects always hold true if, like here, they are sincere and real.

5

ANCENIS

24 miles NE of Nantes

The Romans, who appreciated all that this charming little town had to offer, particularly enjoyed coming to a place that was far from the noise and cares of *Condevincum* (Nantes). Did they appreciate its wine, even in those far-distant days? This was, after all, the period of *Pax Romana,* but it was not to last. The vineyards were ransacked on at least two occasions, in 577 and 593 A.D., during the reign of Clotaire I.

Ancenis, a Breton town on the borders of Brittany and Anjou, had **a feudal castle,** built in the late 10th century; the English took it by storm in 1214. A few years later, it was the turn of King Louis IX of France to establish his sovereignty here. Yet the town retained some of its privileges, in particular exemption from the salt tax. Which immediately brings to mind the very active smuggling trade that soon developed.

All that remains of the **castle** is one bastion, two machicolated towers (15th century), a Renaissance residence (1535) and 17th-century pavilions. It was here, in 1488, that Duke François II of Brittany met King Louis XI of France in order to prepare the treaty that would annex Brittany to the Kingdom of France, the Breton army having been defeated in Saint-Aubin-du-Cormier (12 miles south of Fougères). It was also in this castle that, in 1598, the preparatory talks were held that were to pave the way for the **Edict of Nantes** promulgated on 13th April of that same year.

The fortified castle entrance.

6

La Contrie Manor in Couffe.

Montrelais, the main window. ▶

The French Revolution resulted in the death of many local people (more than one thousand). They were either drowned in the Loire or massacred in the streets and houses by the troops led by the Republican General François Westermann.

With the return of peace, Ancenis licked its wounds and extended the vineyards that now produce an "appellation contrôlée", **Coteaux d'Ancenis** including *Pinot de Loire* and Malmsey for whites and *Cabernet* and *Gamay* for reds and rosés.

Nor is the town devoid of interest for tourists. In addition to the ruins of the castle, the **Rue des Tonneliers** has some fine 18th-century mansions. They once belonged to the wine merchants whose hefty barges and river craft could transport hundreds of barrels of wine in one trip.

St. Peter's Church (église Saint-Pierre), which was altered on several occasions, has a 15th-century belltower-portal topped by a campanile (16th century). The interior, with its modern stained glass windows, houses 17th-century reredos and white marble medallions dating from the 18th century. The statue of St. Peter is 14th century. The ribbed vaulting in the side chapels dates from the 16th century and is very well-preserved. There are a number of interesting sculptures in the **Chapel of Our Lady of Deliverance** near the church. As for the **Davrays Convent** (17th century), all that remains is the arching from its cloisters and the pilastered chapel. A company of riot police now occupies the place which once resounded to the voices of the Ursuline sisters.

The journalist and art critic, Michel Maison, was born in Ancenis in 1923.

Nearby is **Saint-Géréon,** noteworthy for the **Ecochère Estate** and the **Château de la Chevasnerie** which has a park full of trees and tropical plants as well as an orangery.

Not far away is **Couffé** and **La Contrie Manor,** the birthplace of the Royalist General Charette in 1763.

The 280-hectare **Grée Marshes** to the north-east have been delightfully landscaped as a **leisure centre,** but they are also popular with scholars because they are the haunt of migratory birds and have some interesting lakeside plants.

If you cross the suspension bridge (1953), you will find yourself in Anjou, in **Liré** of which the poet Joachim du Bellay (1522-1560) nostalgically sang the praises in a few well-known lines :

"How much more beautiful my Loire than the Latin Tiber, How much more beautiful my little Liré than the Palatine Hills, How much more beautiful than the sea air is the gentle air of Anjou".

The manor that once belonged to the du Bellay family, opposite the church, is now a **museum.** Yet the poet was born several miles away, in a now-ruined manorhouse called **La Turmelière,** on the road to Drain.

Back across the Loire is **Montrelais,** not far from **Varades,** where the main window (1535) in **St. Peter's Church** is a masterpiece of Breton architecture. Incidentally, Montrelais once had the only coalmine in Brittany but it was closed down in 1911.

The seven deadly sins - a keystone in St.Winwaloe's Church.

BATZ-SUR-MER

5 miles SW of Guérande

Between Le Croisic and Le Pouliguen on one side and the coast and saltmarshes on the other, lies the pleasant little town of Batz-sur-Mer with its **harbour** nestling behind a breakwater and an age-old history that goes back to the days when Alain Barbe-Torte, who chased the Vikings out of Nantes c. 936 A.D., gave the land to monks from the famous Abbey of Landévennec 30 miles north of Quimper. The monks turned the estate into a priory and retained ownership of both land and buildings until the French Revolution.

The 13th-century chapel was replaced by St. Guénolé's Church, which was altered on several occasions, the most important being in the 15th, 16th and 17th centuries when a new 195-foot belltower replaced the original one that had been struck by lightning. From the top of the tower, after a climb up a narrow stone staircase, you can see right across the Guérande area and down to the headland at Le Croisic.

The Folk Museum in Batz-sur-Mer.

Among other interesting features, the church contains four keystones representing Christ dressed in animal skins and carrying His Cross, a man lying on his back with his stomach ripped open being attacked by the monsters of the seven deadly sins, the veil of the Holy Face, St. Veronica's veil, held by three angels, and St. Barbara in her tower. A carving on one of the capitals shows a mermaid with long hair flowing down her back. The statue of Our Lady of the Precious Blood dates from the 15th century. In the chancel are some fine gilded wooden altar screens (17th century). The organ was built in the 18th century.

The attractive 15th and 16th-century Gothic chapel of Our Lady of the Thorn Bush (Notre-Dame du Mûrié), of which unfortunately only the walls and pillars are still standing, has a threefold history, or legend, attached to it. Tradition has it that the chapel was built after Lord Yves de Rieux de Ranrouët had made a vow. Caught in a storm when he was returning home from England to marry the beautiful Isolde, he promised the Virgin Mary that, if he escaped safe and well, he would have a chapel built in Her honour on the spot where he landed. This was duly done. The second version recounts how a burning thorn bush guided his lordship back to port. The third version has it that the chapel has nothing to do with a thorn bush and that the "mûrier" in question is only salt water. The word is said to have been derived from the Breton word **mor** (meaning "mer" or "sea") which is often pronounced **mour.** And the word "mourié" means water saturated with salt, in fact the sort of paste-like substance that you can see in the salt-pans. This would hardly be surprising given that Breton was still spoken in Batz-sur-Mer in the years after the First World War. Notre-Dame-du-Mûrier, then, would really mean "Our Lady of Salt Water".

In the street leading to the station is the **Cross of Pain,** carved out of a menhir and now built into the wall of a modern house. It was said to cure rheumatism. Another **menhir,** nearly 10 ft. tall, stands near the Saint-Michael Beach and is said to conceal the treasure once stolen from the Fairy Grotto near Le Pouliguen (q.v.). In Bourg-de-Batz, as you can see, nobody really knows where legend ends and history begins because mysteries and marvels are everywhere, to the delight of the children.

The majestic ruins of Notre-Dame-du-Mûrier (opposite).

The bay at La Baule (pages 14-15).

12

Along the promenade, the architecture is elegant... or audacious (opposite).

LA BAULE-ESCOUBLAC

16 miles W of Saint-Nazaire

"The finest beach in Europe" is a crescent of fine sand stretching over nearly 5 miles from Pornichet to Le Pouliguen. The high promenade running along its entire length was built in 1910.

This seaside resort, which is one of the largest in France, was "discovered" by the people of Nantes c. 1850 and they began to build holiday homes there. Yet it did not really develop on a large scale until 1880. And the arrival of mass tourism has totally changed the resort's appearance with its pinewoods, luxury flats, international hotels, racecourse, and golf courses. There's plenty to add to the enjoyment of summer holidaymakers apart from swimming in the sea.

Escoublac is the new village that replaced the one which disappeared beneath the waves in the 18th century. The permanent population of 15,000 in this Armorican resort, many of them retired people, greatly appreciate the mild climate of "Brittany's dry area" - during the low season, of course, for the summer months bring in floods of visitors.

Yet in his **"Voyage pittoresque en Loire-Inférieure"** written c. 1820, Edouard Richer saw these resorts in a quite different, not to say sinister, light. **"Ever-moving dunes with rugged crests... Arid ridges dominating even more arid valleys... A land devoid of vegetation where all is dead... Visitors find themselves alone between a deserted beach and abandoned sand dunes".** But with a change of century comes a change of scene, and each new era has its own point of view.

The artist Jean Bruneau was born in La Baule in 1921.

BESNE

3 miles S of Pontchâteau

In the local graveyard stands one of the finest **Celtic crosses** (a cross within a circle) in Brittany, also recognised as being among the oldest. It serves as a reminder of the famous circular amulet worn by the Celts and the same theme is also present in the **carillon drums** that are to be found in a few of Brittany's churches, in particular in Confort-en-Meillars in Finistère and, in the Côtes-du-Nord, in Notre-Dame-du-Ruellou, Laniscat, and Kérien.

The **crypt** of the church contains two stone coffins dating from Roman times. Nearby is a **sacred spring** whose waters still flow to this day. A dolmen known as the **Pierre-à-Berthe** was said to relieve the pain of the afflicted who rubbed themselves against it. It was destroyed by its owner c. 1850 because he thought there was buried treasure beneath it. The story does not say whether he even found enough to cover his expenses. The belief in dolmens and menhirs as sites of treasure troves was widespread throughout Brittany. It was said that the "korrigans" or Little People were able to store their fabulous riches underground beneath the stones. Which leads inevitably to thoughts of Snow-White and the Seven Dwarfs.

Gavre Forest.

BLAIN

22 miles N of Nantes

This large community, with a population of almost 7,500, lies practically at the centre of the *"département"*. The **Gâvre Forest** (4,500 hectares) and the nearby **Groulais Forest** give it a magnificent natural setting, and it is crossed by the beautiful river Isac and the Nantes-Brest Canal. As in days gone by, the restful Gâvre Forest is filled with stags and does, roe deer, and wild boar.

Blain existed at least as far back as Gallo-Roman times, as demonstrated by remains that are now kept in a **museum** on the square beside the church. And there were two Roman roads linking the town to Vannes and Rennes.

A fortress was built on the left bank of the R.Isac, probably on

Two views of the museum in Blain (opposite).

the orders of Olivier II de Clisson. But it is to his grandson, Olivier IV, that we owe most of the present castle (1378-1385) with its long, elegant Renaissance facade (it underwent yet another alteration c.1920 when the Prince of Greece was its owner). There are also two mighty towers and ramparts.

Of the nine original towers in the castle, Cardinal de Richelieu had seven demolished. He could not forgive Duke Henri de Rohan, lord of the manor at that time, for his conversion to the Protestant faith and the castle served as a mighty bastion for those of the Reformed Religion. The Rohan family was to retain ownership of the castle from 1407 to 1802.

During the French Revolution, the castle was used by the Republican soldiers as a barracks, while the Royalist troops used it as a prison. This no doubt saved it from total destruction.

Blain Castle (opposite).

BOURGNEUF-EN-RETZ
26 miles SW of Nantes

For many years, the bay at Bourgneuf was known as the **Baye de Bretagne** because the borders of Brittany and Poitou were so imprecise.

Although Bourgneuf-en-Retz now lies 2 miles inland in the midst of the polders, it used to be a **major port** exporting sea salt to Spain, Holland, and England in particular. It was also marked on the Genoese "portulans" (the charts of the day) in the same way as Nantes.

The **church** contains a fine 15th-century crucifix. A 17th-century house has been turned into the **local museum** (musée du Pays de Retz), which is well worth a visit.

The museum in Bourgneuf.

Along canal banks...

... and through villages. ▶

THE BRIÈRE MARSHES
9 miles NE of Saint-Nazaire

In addition to the 6,700 hectares of real marshland, the Brière has now become the **Grande Brière,** a huge regional park covering 40,000 hectares. It is the haunt of numerous species of migratory bird and the canals are filled not only with fish but also with the undulating forms of the "pimpereaux", the local word for eels. This is also a paradise for hunters.

Built on outcrops of granite are a few hamlets and villages. The **Island of Fédrun** has become the

Park's administrative centre and includes the **Bride's House** and **a Brière Cottage** set out as it used to be. But in fact all the houses are thatched cottages. In **Saint-Malo-de-Guersac** there is a zoo and the Lockkeeper's House. The marshes round the main town, **Saint-Joachim,** cover the site of a former channel dating back to the far-off days when Guérande was an island.

There are 21 communities in all, administered by 21 councils. Since time immemmorial, the people of the Brière have defended their privileges, or at least they have since they were granted letters patent by Duke François II of Brittany in 1461, letters which

were later confirmed by successive kings of France.

The locals no longer earn their money from the peat trade which, along with reeds for thatching, used to be one of their traditional sectors of employment. They have now turned their hand to tourism, or goose- and duck-farming, while others go elsewhere to work, mainly to Saint-Nazaire.

There are those who like the Brière and those who do not. It all depends on the time of day, the season of the year, the view, and the mood of the visitor. For Edouard Richer, **"There is nothing more desolate than this area when crossed in the summer months. A heavy, sultry**

An aerial view of the island of Fédrun.

Three views of the Brière Marshes.

atmosphere hangs about you like a cloak…" Yet Alphonse de Chateaubriant described it as **"A great wild marsh stretching into infinity, full of the silence of man and the song of the birds, where spreading out great wings as white as snow and gliding between the flowers on the water are the punts cutting through the splendid air tinged with sunshine"**.

In fact, despite appearances, the entire area is filled with "magic" thanks to its folk tales and legends. And if you are ever told that the **"blins"** (the flat-bottomed boats) of the local people are sometimes escorted at night by strange lights,

they are the souls that wander over the surface of the water. Not just any souls but those of the men sacrificed in olden days by the Druids… Luckily the golden sparkle of the sunrise soon sheds its splendour across the entire landscape.

A hide.

CHATEAUBRIANT

39 miles NE of Nantes

Once upon a time there was a man named Brient. The "once" in question is the 11th century. And Brient I built a fortress which was mentioned in the parchments of the day as *castellum Brient,* hence the later name, Châteaubriant. Yet the town was called *Montagne-sur-Chère* until 1795, the Chère being a delightful little river that flows through the district.

At present, the **castle** has two parts. All that remains of the old **fortress** is a **square keep.** The second section, known as the **new castle,** was built for Count Jean de Laval. It is a fine **Renaissance palace** (1533-1539) with elegant colonnades and arches forming a stark contrast when seen from the courtyard.

Of the castle's residents over the years, the famous Françoise de Foix attracted more than the passing notice of King François I of France. Much was said about the love affair of François and Françoise. Tradition has it that Françoise was murdered on her jealous husband's orders but there is no historical basis for this tale since Françoise was still alive at least eleven years after the supposed date of the murder. It is also said that she returns to her beautiful residence from time to time, when the roses come into bloom.

The Renaissance wing of the chateau.

The main staircase with coffered ceiling.

The bartizan in the feudal section of the castle (above).

The chevet of the church of Saint-Jean-de-Béré (opposite).

St. Nicholas' Church in the town centre is a 19th-century building. Much older is the **Church of St. John of Béré** in the suburb of the same name (11th-12th centuries with 17th-century alterations). The south wall is decorated with carved bas-reliefs dating from the 13th and 16th centuries ; the wooden porch is 15th century. Inside, there are a number of interesting statues (15th and 17th centuries), and some fine 17th-century marble altars. Every year in September, Béré is the setting for a lively **fair.** Châteaubriant itself has a large cattle market.

The Vioreau Dam.

Saint-Jean-de-Béré : the south porch (opposite, top).

La Blissière Lake (opposite, bottom).

The town contains several **old houses,** in particular in the Rue du Couéré where there are three dating from the 15th century, including the **Angel's House.**

In the early days of the German occupation, 40,000 prisoners were held in four camps nearby. The one in Choiseul lost 36 hostages who were taken out and shot in La Blisière and La Sablière. There is a **memorial** to them in La Sablière.

The entire Châteaubriant area, the so-called **Mée Region,** has much to offer tourists. There is a wide choice of sights and places to visit, ranging from the Araize, Juigné, Teillé, Saffré, Arche, and Saint-Mars Forests, the lakes at Gravetel, La Forge, La Blisière and Le Pin, or the Vioreau Lake that is so well-known to anglers. On the banks of the R.Don stands the proud outline of the **Château de la Motte-Glain,** with its two pepperpot towers. It houses a **Hunting Museum** and, in the summer, is used for cultural events. The 13th-century **chapel** in **Saint-Aubin-des-Châteaux** once belonged to the Knights Templar. Not far away is the **Louères Men-hir,** also known as the Louée Menhir, said to be a piece of gravel that fell out of Gargantua's sandal. If you put your ear to it, you will hear the hours striking - or so runs the tale. **Villepot Church** has a particularly attractive black marble and limestone reredos (1692) which deserves to be better known.

Châteaubriant, where Victor Hugo's mother, Sophie Trébuchet, lived for a few years, was also the birthplace of the poet Yves Cosson, who wrote :

"Our childhood leaves behind a scent of velvet for eternity".

33

Clisson Castle.

The entrance and inner courtyard of the Château de la Motte-Glain.

CLISSON

17 miles SE of Nantes

The fortress in Clisson was believed to be impregnable because of its sheer size - this proved to be untrue. It lay in a very exposed position and, standing as it did on the marches of Brittany, Anjou and Poitou, it excited the envy of many a warring faction.

Yet between the bitter struggles of the Middle Ages and the carnage of the French Revolution, the original 13th-century **castle** was altered by Duke François II of Brittany. He made it his principal residence, and gave sumptuous receptions there in honour of his wife, Margaret of Foix. During the Revolution, though, fierce fighting between Republicans and Royalists left nothing but ruins, albeit still filled with a sense of grandeur.

An obliging guide will show you the outer walls flanked by a number of machicolated towers and protected by a double moat, the remains of the chapel, the kitchens, the great residence restored by Olivier de Clisson - and the famous well in the inner courtyard which was filled with the bodies of unfortunate royalists in 1794. You can also see the Elm Bastion, the square keep (15th century), and two round towers at the end of the courtyard which were used as a prison for many years. One of them now houses a **Museum of Arts and Crafts.**

During the Revolution, the town itself was not spared for it was set ablaze from one end to the other on the orders of the Republican General Turreau, the organiser of the **"fearsome columns"** which crossed Vendée. Only the covered market (15th-18th centuries) escaped unscathed.

With the return of peace, two wealthy men from Nantes named François and Pierre Cacault began

A panoramic view of Clisson (above).

*A steep narrow alleyway
in Old Clisson (opposite).*

rebuilding the town, with the assistance of Frédéric Lemot, a sculptor from Lyons. The reconstruction was in the Florentine style which has left us today with a delightful **Italianate community** with orange roofs of Roman-type tiles, square houses with balconies, steep alleyways, and flights of irregular steps. The town's patrons added a Roman house and a church, also in the Italian style, on the site of the old collegiate church. The two bridges across the rivers Sèvre and Moine are much, much older.

The covered market (opposite).
The R. Sèvre Nantaise
near Boussay (overleaf).

Clisson has three **Romanesque sanctuaries** built in the style of the Poitou School - the Madeleine (12th century), St. James' (12th century) and Holy Trinity (11th-12th centuries). The first of them now lies in ruins ; the second has become a youth club.

Despite its past misfortunes, Clisson has become so attractive that it has justly, and through its proud motto "For whatever pleases me", been nicknamed the "French Tivoli", with its parasol pines and the beautiful quality of light that is so particular to the Loire Valley.

Two views of the harbour.

LE CROISIC

6 miles W of La Baule

Le Croisic, a very attractive seaside resort with a bustling **harbour,** was famous as far back as the 16th century for its exports of sea salt from Guérande and Mesquer. Yet its origins are even older for St. Felix, the great Bishop of Nantes, came here to christen the last of the Veneti to be converted to Christianity. The ceremony was held on the spot where the **Crucifix Chapel** was built in later years (16th century).

Given a geographical position that would now be described as strategic, Le Croisic was subjec-ted to numerous sieges and attacks until the 17th century.

Another old chapel, **St. Gous-**

Aerial views of the harbour and peninsula at Le Croisic (opposite).

tan's, between the harbour and the Pointe du Croisic, used to be a place of pilgrimage. Sailors' wives would come here to pray on stormy days. Nearby, there was a spring believed to cure ills. In the centre of the old town of Le Croisic is the **Church of Our Lady of Pity** (15th century), which has a late 17th-century lantern tower and several very old statues including one of **Our Lady of the Winds.** The Virgin Mary holds the Infant Jesus in her left arm while in her right hand she carries a compass. At the end of the harbour and the fishmarket is the **Aiguillon Residence** (17th-18th centuries). Its facade is decorated with Corinthian columns, and it now houses the Town Hall and the

Navy Museum. Other 15th- and 16th-century houses line the Rue de l'Eglise, while the Rue du Pilor contains the particularly attractive **Limur Residence** (1613). A sight not to be missed on the Quai Port-Cignet is the remarkable **Coast of Love Aquarium.**

From **Mont Lénigo** at the mouth of the harbour, the view stretches right across the bay from Pembron to the Pointe du Castelli.

And this being Brittany, it has to be said that, for many years, a dead priest used to celebrate Mass before a congregation of the deceased in the **Crucifix Chapel.** The event always took place at night, those Breton nights which belonged to "those from elsewhere" as soon as darkness fell.

DONGES
30 miles W of Nantes

On the banks of the R.Loire, the town of Donges, the main town in the Brière region, is now famous for its great **refineries** which grew up around the harbour in the estuary catering for giant tankers.

All that remains of its past is the ruined church that was once part of **Notre-Dame Priory.** Rebuilt after the war, the parish church has a square tower and the West Front is carved in traditional Breton style.

The entire region along the estuary, with **Montoir,** is gradually being transformed and marshland is being reclaimed to

In the background, the fishmarket in Le Croisic.

La Chantrerie.

provide space for the companies that will make this a major industrial estate and harbour. The development is vital if the area is to face up to the necessities of the near future.

THE ERDRE VALLEY CASTLES

North of Nantes

Beyond **Mazerolles Lake,** the R. Erdre becomes the beautiful waterway that was appreciated even in the days of the Marquise de Sévigné. And the people of Nantes appreciate it for its charm that is further enhanced by towns, castles and wooded footpaths. This is an area of tranquillity, harmony, and beauty that is particu-

La Gâcherie.

43

larly suitable for healthful relaxation.

Apart from the villages of **Nort-sur-Erdre** and **Sucé,** which we shall describe in detail further on, there is a succession of attractive estates and castles, many of them standing in the midst of magnificent parks. Going upstream, you can see **L'Eraudière,** a 16th-century manorhouse, the **Beaujoire** exhibition centre and park that are used for the International Flower Festival, **La Chanterie, La Couronnerie and La Châtaigneraie** on the left bank. On the right bank are **La Desnerie** with its Louis XIII façade, **La Poterie, La Gâcherie** (15th century) which received the visit of the Queen of Navarre in 1537 and was the country seat of the Marquisate of Charette in 1775, the **Château de Naye** and many other, less prestigious but no less noteworthy country houses.

All these wonderful buildings can be admired fully in their setting of trees and parkland, if you take a boat trip from **Le Petit Port,** quai de Versailles, in Nantes.

FÉGRÉAC
*6 miles N of
Saint-Gildas-des-Bois*

This village with its population of approximately 1,800 is no longer what it was during the Roman occupation when it was called **Duretie** and, with its 30,000 inhabitants, was the second largest town in Brittany. The territory included **Rieux** and the two towns formed a single extensive conurbation containing a major road junction with roads leading to Nantes, Angers, and Quimper.

There was a ford across the R.Vilaine at Rieux. The town also lay on the edge of the territories of various Gallic tribes i.e. the Curiosolites, the Veneti, and the Namneti. **Archaeological digs** in both Rieux and Fégréac have uncovered large remains such as arenas, a temple dedicated to Minerva, Roman baths, hostelries, and villas.

GUÉRANDE
50 miles W of Nantes

An unbroken line of ramparts (14th and 15th centuries) protects the old town of Guérande. Ten **towers** are spaced out along the walls and there are four **gates.** An additional attraction for visitors is the fact that all the fortifications are intact. War passed the town

An aerial view of the marshes (pages 46-47).

A saltpan worker.

The St. Michael Gate.

by ; yet it was in the very thick of things in the 10th century when the people of Guérande repulsed an attack by the Vikings.

The town, which was once a major political and trading centre thanks to the salt marshes, has succeeded in maintaining and increasing its cultural influence and its share of the tourist industry. Visitors enjoy strolling through its **mediaeval streets,** entering the well-stocked **Old Guérande Museum** housed in **St. Michael's Gate,** and walking round **St. Aubin's Church** (9th, 14th and 16th centuries) where the capitals depict hilarious little devils going about their evil business on an obviously uncomfortable group of the damned. Like St. Aubin's Church, **the Chapel of Our White Lady** has ribbed vaulting.

Yet the town attracts not only large numbers of tourists but also artists, craftsmen, musicians, and actors, because cultural events show an upsurge each year. The historian and poet Pierre de La Condamine is the editor of the wonderful *Cahiers du Pays de Guérande.*

Major plays are staged in the **Château de Careil** on the road to La Baule. After being set on fire by Leaguers on 11th May 1589, this 16th-century fortress was rebuilt in the Renaissance style.

And on the road to La Roche-Bernard, you can see the **Devil's Mill** where, or so the story goes,

Lucifer was tricked. A fairly common occurence in tales and legends ; much less so in reality.

In the depths of the salt marshes lies the village of **Saillé,** which still has traditional houses with limewashed walls and blue-tinted slate roofs. The workers from the marshes still wear their unusual traditional costume for the religious procession held on St. Claire's Day in October. Young girls wear white dresses ; married women are dressed in purple. Their aprons are a shimmering bronze and the bibs are embroidered with gold and silver thread. Their stockings are red. The men wear several waistcoats, one on top of the other, all of them open and decorated with rich colours.

Guérande and its old town walls.

The Devil's Mill. ▶

Underneath is a white waistcoat, worn buttoned up, trimmed with red and black. Their wide pleated breeches are made of white linen. They also wear a sort of sweeping Spanish-style cape. Their wide-brimmed hats are made of felt and the brim is turned up at the side if the man is a bachelor. Married men turn theirs up at the front; widowers at the back. The women's head-dresses consist of lace pinners with a pleated base.

And here you find all the magic of **salt.** This is where seawater undergoes its transformation, in the marshes of Guérande and Mesquer. The sea gushes into the marshes along a network of canals called *"étiers"*. It then flows from one compartment to the next, taking its time as it does so, in a movement that is invisible to the naked eye. The deepest compartments, approximately 5ft. in depth, are at the beginning of the network of channels. These are the mudflats and saltpans and the water starts to evaporate at this stage. The other compartments, the so-called *"adernes"* or *"oeillets"* (evaporating pans), are much more shallow, with a depth of only 2 to 4 inches. It is here that the last of the water finally evaporates, leaving behind nothing but a pure white product called "prime salt". The worker collects the salt using a sort of long-handled wooden rake known as the *"rouable"* or *"las"*. He then piles it up on the rounded platforms that separate the saltpans before carrying it to a different spot near the marsh where he adds it to a large pile of salt called a *"mulon"*. This, then, is how we acquire this fine gift of the sun and the sea.

Grand-Lieu Lake (photo by H. Cayeux).

GRAND-LIEU LAKE
12 miles SW of Nantes

Swollen by the winter rains, three rivers in the Retz area (the Logne, Boulogne and Oignon) provide Grand-Lieu Lake with such a large quantity of water that it forms the largest stretch of inland water in France, with a total area of between 6,000 and 7,500 hectares. In the summer months, the lake still has some of the water but most of it has changed into marshland and swamps covered with reeds and has become the haunt of migratory birds, fish and frogs. After the Brière to the north-west on the other bank of the Loire, this is the second largest "breath of fresh air" for the region as a whole. The best view of the lake is to be had from near

the tiny harbour at **Passay.** A fourth river, the Acheneau, links the lake to the R.Loire, but only in certain seasons because, depending on the water level in the lake itself, the river changes direction.

Numerous tales have made the lake famous, among them the tragic story of **Herbauge,** a town which disappeared beneath its waters in the 6th century because of the immoral behaviour of its inhabitants. Only one virtuous family was granted permission to flee - and then only on condition that nobody turned round. Unfortunately, the wife was too inquisitive and was instantly changed into a standing stone known as **St.Martin's Stone** which can still be seen near the village of Cheix. This, of course, is reminiscent of

the story of Sodom and Gomorrha. Yet what is more certain that, nowadays, the area provides visitors with a chance to enjoy peace, tranquillity and relaxation.

HERBIGNAC
37 miles NW of Nantes

The town lies on a rise surrounded by moorland and marshes. It is a good tourist centre to the north-west of the Brière, in an area filled with **dolmens** and **standing stones.**

Those who like pottery, indeed professional potters, will be interested in the two-hundred-year-old kilns in a pottery in **Landieul** - although they are really of interest to one and all.

Not far away is **Ranrouët Castle** (12th-15th and 17th centuries), an impressive sight already and destined to be even more so once the restoration work has been completed. A moat surrounds the outer walls. An arched gateway with narrow coving leads to the vast inner courtyard. From the top of the six towers, it was easy to keep watch on the entire northern sector of the Guérande Peninsula. The garrison could include anything up to 300 men and 100 horses. The castle was demolished in 1616 and rebuilt in 1639. During the French Revolution, 60 royalists withstood a four-month siege by 20,000 Republican soldiers, then the castle was set on fire.

To the north of **Saint-Lyphard** are some strange remains of the days of the Roman legions - deep trenches that were dug on the orders of Julius Caesar in an attempt to contain the turbulent Veneti within the natural boundaries of the Brière.

The poet René-Guy Cadou (1920-1951) was born in **Sainte-Reine-de-Bretagne** which boasts two **dolmens** and the ruins of **Crévy Castle.**

In **La Chapelle-des-Marais,** as elsewhere and in particular in Carnac and Saint-Herbot, there used to be a procession in honour of St. Cornély. At the end of the procession, which was held in September, all the oxen were blessed. Worth visiting here are the **Traditional Arts and Crafts Centre** and the **Clogmaker's House.**

LE LOROUX-BOTTEREAU
12 miles E of Nantes

This town with a population in excess of 4,000 existed far back in history and once had a castle of which the 15th-century ruins can still be seen near a small lake. The Romanesque St. Lawrence's Chapel was even older (12th century) but no longer exists. It used to contain **frescoes** which are now in the parish church. The **bells** are among the finest in France.

Note that the main square has, since 1823, boasted one of the very, very few statues of Louis XVI still in existence.

The history of **La Chapelle-Basse-Mer** to the north-west was subjected to meticulous research

The Château de Ranrouët.

The front and interior of Haute-Goulaine.

The Château de Haute-Goulaine contains an aviary that is as unexpected as it is extravagant, with an admirable collection of butterflies.

by Reynald Secher in 1986, especially with regard to events during the French Revolution. And it's true that the entire region suffered badly throughout this period, as we have already seen in Clisson.

The **Château de Haute-Goulaine** still belongs to the Goulaine family which commissioned its building in the 15th century. After a recent restoration project, it is now justifiably considered as one of the famous **Loire Valley castles** with its mainly Renaissance facade of stone-mullioned windows and unusual dormer windows, its elegant corner tower, and two very fine staircase towers. The château was built on the site of a feudal castle which had belonged to the same family since the 10th century. Marquis Robert de Goulaine is also a "writer of mystery stories" in addition to fulfilling his role as Grand Master of the Order of the Wine-tasting Knights of Brittany, a bacchic brotherhood whose motto is *"Drink the wine and be as good as it is"*. Quite a tall order.

And there is a tale of fantasy attached to **Barbechat.** The Devil is said to have swallowed a lively cat that had preceded him across the Louen Bridge in the Goulaine Marshes. The Devil's throat is said to be suffering from the scratches to this day.

MACHECOUL

24 miles SW of Nantes

This is the main town in the Retz area, and a major cattle and horse-breeding centre. It also has a flourishing vegetable and flower trade among other industries, including mechanical engineering. The town still has a number of **old houses,** one dating from the 15th century, while the law courts (17th-18th centuries) have now become the Town Hall.

And on the banks of the R. Falleron stands the **keep** of the mighty castle built by the lords of Retz in the 14th century. It was here that the infamous Gilles de Rais committed many of his crimes before being strung up then burnt at the stake in Nantes on 26th October 1440 at the age of 36.

In the **Machecoul Marshes,** it is easy to imagine the difficult life of the peasants in bygone days, in hovels that were often surrounded by water after heavy winter rain.

The writer and journalist Henri de Grandmaison was born in Machecoul in 1933.

To the south-west stands the **Quinquénavant Chapel,** a Romanesque building of the Poitou School (12th century) with an 11th-century crypt. Another such 12th-century Romanesque chapel can be seen in **Touvois.**

It was from **Fonteclose Manor** that François de Charette set out to lead the bitter struggle against the Republicans before being captured by General Hoche and shot in Nantes, at the age of 33, on 29th March 1796.

The keep at Machecoul.

Meilleraye Abbey.

LA MEILLERAYE-DE-BRETAGNE

27 miles N of Nantes

It is somewhat of an understatement to say that the **Perron Dolmen** at the northern end of the Arche Forest, also known as the **Gallic Stone,** does not have the best of reputations, especially at nightfall. The **Béré Beast** haunts the area and the mere sight of this evil creature causes immediate death, so that nobody has ever been able to describe it. It is, of course, a monster from the world of the supernatural but, all the same, in the winter when the storms blow up from the nor'west.....

Much more restful is the Cistercian **Abbey** of La Meilleraye, or Melleray, which stands near a small lake between the Vioreau and Ancenis Forests. It was founded in 1145 and the church, which was consecrated in 1183, still has its original nave. The West Front was rebuilt in the 15th century, the chancel in the late 19th. The tower dates from the 14th century. The vast library is open to the public but the church is only open on Sundays and holidays of obligation, during services.

Occupied by a congregation of Trappist monks, the abbey is the best-known in the county and far beyond.

A reredos in the church in Missillac

The tiny church in Prigny and its reredos (opposite)

MISSILLAC
15 miles SW of Redon

Mirrored in a delightful lake against a splendid background of trees and lawns stands the elegant **Château de la Bretesche,** in the heart of the Missillac area to the north-east of the Grande Brière. Its Renaissance towers have stood here since they were first built for Jean de Laval in the 18th century. And the rural setting comprises no less than 200 hectares laid out as a golf course and equestrian cen-

tre. The outbuildings have been turned into a hotel.

War is no respecter of masterpieces and this château suffered fire damage during the Revolution. Luckily, it was restored in the 19th and 20th centuries. And it is often hard to tear oneself away from it.

MOISDON-LA-RIVIÈRE
7 miles S of Châteaubriant

Perhaps it would now be more correct to speak of **Moisdon-les-Rivières** in the plural since the

town with a population of some 1,800 now stretches from the R.Don to the R.Gravotel. Singular or plural, however, this is a pleasant area to visit, with a plethora of lakes and woods.

First on the list of sights is the town itself. **St. Jouan's Church** was built in the Romanesque style and fortified in the 15th century. The spire dates from the 18th century. And the wonderful **Forge-Neuve Folk Museum,** which is housed in a 17th-century building, gives a lot of information about the local foundries.

LES MOUTIERS

27 miles SW of Nantes

The town gets its name from the two religious communities that used to exist here, one opposite the other on what is now the main square - **St. Peter's Priory** for the monks and **Notre-Dame Priory** for the nuns. **St. Peter's Church** includes certain features of the original priory, said to date back to the 11th century. The West Door dates from the 16th century. On the spot where Notre-Dame Priory once stood, there is now a statue of the Madonna and Child flanked by two yew trees.

People also come to Les Moutiers to see the **Lantern of the Deceased.** It stands in front of the church, a small round tower with an altar built into its walls at the top of two steps. The tower has a stone Cross at the top and a staircase inside. It is almost 5 ft. in diameter and is 23 ft. high. A fire is traditionally lit in it after a death in the parish, as well as during the night of the 1st/2nd November.

This tradition preceded Christianity. For the Ancient Celts, too, fire was a symbol of death and resurrection, as well as representing **Bel, Belen,** or **Beler,** the great sun god. Neither are the yews to each side of the statue of the Madonna and Child just any tree. The yew represents the Celtic god **Ivin,** protector of the deceased, and its planting was part of a ritual held early in December. It's hardly surprising, then, that there are yew trees in so many cemeteries ; the custom goes far back into the mists of time.

The Lantern of the Deceased (top).
Votive offerings from seamen (bottom).

NANTES

65 miles S of Rennes

The last census showed a population of 247,227. This, of course, is quite different to the 13,000 to 20,000 inhabitants in the 3rd-century town. Those were the days of the Roman Occupation when the town was already one of the most important administrative and trading centres in Gaul. Capital of the Gallic Namneti tribe, it was then known as **Condevincum.**

Over the centuries its position at the mouth of the R.Loire with the ocean to the east and access inland by means of the same waterway enabled it to enjoy continual expansion despite numerous wars. It was the subject of battles involving, in succession, the Romans, Bretons, Franks, Attila and his Huns, Saxons and Vikings. The latter took shelter on the islands and in the marshes that then covered most of the area and stayed there for one hundred years, until driven out by the Breton chieftain Alain Barbetorte. In the meantime, they had sailed up the Loire into Auvergne, ransacking and pillaging everything in their way. In Nantes (**Naoned,** in Breton), they had massacred Bishop Gohard and his priests in the cathedral, in addition to many others elsewhere.

Thereafter, the town was, for many years, a trump card in the political struggle opposing France and England. Then came the conflict between France and the Dukes of Brittany, each attempting to ensure the supremacy of his own influence. Finally, during the reign of Louis XI, there came the defeat of Duke François II. The almost forced marriage of Anne of Brittany and Charles VIII, and the Edict of 14th August 1532 made Brittany a French province despite the clauses of the **Act of Union** which was no more than a leaf blown away by the storms of the 1789 Revolution. Yet the town had preeminence over Rennes at administrative level.

It was then that Nantes developed its maritime trade, becoming the largest port in France in the 18th century. A "slave-trading" port, it's true, but not the only one. It was, though, the largest

The castle of the Dukes of Brittany (bottom). The Golden Crown Tower within the castle walls (opposite).

An aerial view of the former Feydeau Island.

The castle and cathedral.

The tiny harbour looks towards the point where the R. Erdre disappears beneath the Cours des 50-Otages. ▶

port in Europe as regards the trade in "ebony wood". Nantes alone provided shipment for 300,000 slaves from Black Africa to the plantations of the Caribbean, to replace the local Indians who had died in epidemics or who were murdered.

The Revolution was initially welcomed in Nantes, but the close proximity of Vendée, which was in revolt, led to a decision by the Convention to send Carrier to the town. From November 1793 to February 1794, he had between 2,000 and 5,000 people drowned and at least 3,000 shot. As many, if not more, died of hunger in the

prisons - if they did not succumb first to typhus. Holidaymakers of today are probably not aware that the French word "baignade" (bathing, swimming) was coined by Carrier for obviously tragic purposes. Likewise, Carrier spoke of the guillotine as the **"national razor"**. He was finally recalled to Paris where he was himself sent to the block on 16th December 1794 during the reactionary days of the Thermidor.

There were other major tragic events in Nantes' history during the Second World War. Hostages were taken and shot, and nearly 2,000 people died while 3,000

were injured in a series of 35 air raids which razed to the ground 2,000 houses and flats and badly damaged 6,000 more. It took ten years to rebuild the town.

The quality of the new style of town planning is as high here as in other towns and cities, but it has preserved the **two old districts** round the cathedral and the ducal castle and along the Quai de la Fosse and the Ile Feydeau. The first of these districts covers the site of the original town but it underwent major alteration and much restoration over the course of the centuries. The second district developped from the 15th

The coving on the central doorway in the cathedral.

The nave in the cathedral. ►

century onwards and attained its architectural heyday in the 18th century when the shipowners had superb mansions built here.

Between these two districts was the R.Erdre, which now flows beneath the Cours des Cinquante-Otages from the **Petit Port** near the county buildings (Préfecturè). Now that several arms of the R.Loire have been filled in, the town no longer bears any resemblance to a **"Little Venice".** Zebra crossings have replaced the fifty bridges still remaining at the turn of the century, many of which had an age-old history. But let's not get carried away by nostalgia ! Town councils have done their best to

preserve the essential features of the urban landscape while catering for the **rolling tide of traffic.** Nantes does not give the impression of being squashed into an area of stone and concrete. The Loire and the many open spaces are still there, ideal settings in which to dream of quiet travel.

St. Peter's Cathedral stands high above the first of these districts. The oldest of its predecssors, built in the 6th century, was said to be the finest church in France. The present building is, in fact, the third on the site. Work began on it in 1434 and was not completed until 1893, i.e. more than five hundred years later. Bet-

ter late than never, as they say. And part of it (the rafters, and the vaulting in the chancel and transept) was damaged by fire on 28th January 1972. The restoration was completed in 1985. Instead of building the cathedral in granite, like its predecessors, it was constructed using white stone. This produced a very beautiful cathedral designed by an architect named Mathelin Rodier in the Flamboyant Gothic style. It has **two towers** rising to 205 ft. and five doorways, three of them decorating the West Front. The statues represent St. Peter, the Virgin Mary and St. Paul. The pillars, moulded in a single block, sup-

A general view and close-up of François II's tomb.

port the vaulting 122 ft. above the ground. And one of the tombs still bears its original name of **the Carmelite Tomb,** which it was given because it was originally sited in the Carmelite chapel. This is the magnificent tomb commissioned by Anne of Brittany, designed by Jean Perréal and carved by Michel Colombe in 1507, to contain the mortal remains of her father, Duke François II and her mother, Margaret of Foix. The sarcophagus is an outstanding example of early 16th-century sculpture. The reclining figures lay on a black marble slab and show a serenity that is unforgettable. Four allegorical figures representing Justice, Prudence, Strength and Temperance, stand at each corner. The statue of Justice, which has delicate features imbued with goodness, is said to be a portrait of Duchess Anne. Beneath the south side of the chancel is a **Romanesque crypt** discovered in 1886. Wonderful new **stained glass windows** were made for the cathedral by Anne Lechevalier and Jean Le Moal.

St. Peter's Gate, on the north side of the cathedral, dates from the 15th century but has Gallo-Roman foundations. It has a tall roof with dormer windows and chimneys. Not far away on the other side of the Cours Saint-Pierre is the Rue Malherbe which leads to the **Chapel of the Immaculate Conception** (15th and 17th centuries but restored in 1849). South of the cathedral stands an elegant manorhouse known as **La Psalette** (1502). It has a multi-faceted tower.

Still in this district, visitors can admire a whole row of 18th-century private mansions lining the **Cours Saint-Pierre** and the **Cours Saint-André,** where it is pleasant to stroll in the shade of the trees. At the top of a column is a statue of Louis XVI, high above the Place Maréchal Foch.

Lower down near the R.Erdre is the **Town Hall,** which really consists of three old private mansions. The **Derval Mansion** (1605) has a Renaissance facade decorated with fluted pilasters, masks and bas-reliefs and includes an elegant arcaded gallery and an unusual slate sundial. The modern wrought-iron grille opening onto the inner courtyard was made by a master ironsmith named Subes. The **Rosmadec Residence** (c. 1563) has a beautiful interior staircase with stone balusters, and a finely-carved ceiling. The front of the **Monti Residence** has four bulls' eye windows on the third floor. Not far from this group of buildings are the 18th-century county buildings

Nantes Town Hall.

(Préfecture), built in an austere Classical style. At one time, the building housed Brittany's Audit Office.

The other main building in this old district is, of course, the **ducal castle.** It was first commissioned in 1207 by Peter of Dreux, Duke of Brittany, and was both completed and refurbished in the 16th century by Duke François II. The work was finished by his daughter, Anne, who had become Queen of France. The main gate is flanked by two massive towers, the **Cabriole** and the **Bakery** (15th century), their walls pierced with slit windows and barred lights. From the vast main courtyard, which contains a fine wrought-iron **well,** there is an admirable view of a large building with four storeys and traceried dormer windows in the Flamboyant Gothic style extending into the **Golden Crown Tower.** Along the south wall is another building with dormer windows and chimneys decorated in the Renaissance style. Opposite the Place de la Duchesse-Anne is the **Horseshoe Tower** and the **River Tower,** linked by a curtain wall. The wide moat, which was once filled directly by the Loire, has been set out as a public park. The impressive keep in the original castle forms a stark contrast to the other features.

This castle is not only attractive to look at ; in its day, it was also a mighty fortress with an artillery battery, under Duke François II, comprising 15 cannon, 16 culverins, 12 arquebuses and 30 brigandines. Receptions were held here in the presence of kings and

The inner courtyard in the castle.

queens but the castle also had a darker role when famous prisoners were incarcerated within its walls, among them Gilles de Retz, Cardinal de Retz, Surintendant Fouquet and Duchess de Berry.

Passing years, warfare, and the requirements of modern town planning have destroyed most of the mediaeval housing. There are only a few examples left, in particular in the Rue de la Juiverie near **Holyrood Church** (église de la Sainte-Croix) in which people pray to Our Lady of Assistance. On the Place du Change, there is

Place du Change.

Rue Baclerie (below).

Rue de la Juiverie (page 73).

an attractive **half-timbered house.**

And here we are, in the second of the old districts, the one bordering the Loire. The main part of it is the **Quai de la Fosse** where thousands of ships tied up over the centuries. Those were the days (especially in the 18th century) when the influential shipowners enjoyed the privilege of wearing a sword. From their windows, they could keep an eye on the work force of four or five thousand dockers and sailors employed there every day, whether they lived on the Quai de la Fosse or on the **Ile Feydeau** opposite where twenty-four shipping magnates had had their mansions built on piles.

The harbour has now become the gigantic **Independent Harbour of Nantes/Saint-Nazaire.** The shipowners' houses have all disappeared except, on the Quai, for the **Darbré Residence, the offices of the French East India Company** and another mansion built in the Louis XV style. The **private mansions** on the Ile Feydeau are in a much better condition, especially those in the Rue Kervegan or the Charron Residence (1727) and **La Villestreux Mansion** on the Place de la Petite-Hollande.

It was this district that used to contain the **shipyards,** the oldest of all Nantes' industries. The timber came from the forests in Central France and was floated down

Quai de la Fosse (above)

The harbour (opposite).

74

Rue Crébillon.

from the Allier. There are locals who still remember the great three-masted sailing ships, and the four-masted Cape Horners arriving from Chili. As the song says,

"Then we're off to Valparaiso
Haul away Ho! Heave ho!
Where others will leave their
bones!
Haul away, matelot! Heave ho!
Pull! Heave ho"...

Not forgetting another eminent erstwhile feature of this area, the transporter bridge which was 620 ft. long with a deck 162 ft. above the river at its highest point. It had a short life - only 55 years.

This leads us into another period of Nantes' history, the 19th century, and another area - the western end of the town, most of which was built to designs by the architect Mathurin Crucy. The **Rue Crébillon** running from the **Place Graslin** to the **Place Royale** is lined with shops large and small, stocked as well as anything you could see in Paris. So what's the use of going to the capital. Take a "stroll along Crébillon", and save time. And on into the Gay Nineties and the Edwardian period with the **Pommeraye Arcade,** a shopping arcade with a wide central staircase leading to three different floors, lined with pillars, statues and medallions. On the **Place Royale,** there is a personalized representation of the R.Loire in the form of a white marble statue carved in 1865 by a sculptor named Driolet. There are also bronze statues of its tributaries. With its circular basin it is a particularly fine fountain. The Gothic architecture of the nearby **St. Nicholas' Church** dates only from 1844 but it was well-designed, by Jean-Baptiste Lassus, the architect in charge of the restoration of the Sainte Chapelle in Paris.

Near the **Place Graslin** and the

The Pommeraye Arcade
(opposite, top)

Place Royale (opposite, bottom)

Cours Cambronne.

The Graslin Theatre.

theatre of the same name is the Cours Cambronne which, in a district that is particularly busy, provides a haven of tranquillity. It is lined with elegantly and austerely grand buildings.

Many of the town's squares are of historic importance. The leader of the Royalist rebels, Cathelineau, was fatally wounded on the **Place Viarme** in 1793, and three years later the Royalist General, Charette de la Contrie, came before the firing squad here. The **Place du Bouffay** was the site of the guillotine during the Revolution. But times pass, and the square is now one of the most attractive in Nantes with its market, stalls and shops. Still very popular, as

Place Mellinet.

always, is the **Place du Commerce,** which has recently been successfully altered. Until the 16th century, it was the **"Wine Harbour".** It owes its present name to the Stock Exchange, now the **Chamber of Commerce,** that closes off one end. The **Place du Pilori** now has little of interest left apart from its name, but then nobody is put in the stocks any more. In Chantenay, a rustic calm reigns in the octagonal **Place Mellinet** lined with identical houses.

As to the open spaces, parks and other such public gardens, the choice is wide. Near the **Gare d'Orléans** (rebuilt in the 60's on the site of an older railway station dating from 1851) are the peaceful **Botanic Gardens** with their numerous rare trees, including several superb magnolias. In the Grand Blottereau, visitors can enter a different world in the vast exotic greenhouses of the **Tropical Gardens.** The charming little

The botanic gardens.

figurehead in the Naval Museum.

Chézine flows through the **Parc e Procé.** Then there is the **quare Elisa-Mercoeur** named honour of a poetess of the omantic period. The **Parc de la audinière** is still the haunt of houghtful swans, while the **Parc e la Beaujoire** hosts the International Flower Festival. And hildren can enjoy a memorable isit to the **Jonelière Zoo.** To the outh, there is an area full of **caves** igh above the R. Sèvre Nantaise.

And so back into town for the bligatory visit to the **museums.** ou can learn a lot and enjoy ourself at the same time because all of them contain treasures amassed by discriminating collectors, benefactors, and patrons, and purchased by successive town councils. Nantes may have had a particular maritime vocation but many of the shipowners and ships' captains were also men of excellent taste.

The ducal castle alone houses the **Maritime Museum,** the **Museum of Popular Arts and Crafts** and the **Art Deco Museum.** At no. 10 Rue Georges-Clémenceau you will find the Art Gallery while the Place Jean V is the site of the **Dobrée Museum** (one of its rooms is devoted entirely to the royalist uprising in Vendée). Then there is the **Jules Verne Museum,** at 3 Rue de l'Hermitage, the **Natural History Museum** in the Rue Voltaire, the **Doll Museum** at 39 boulevard Saint-Aignan, the **Postal Museum** at 3 boulevard Auguste-Pageot, the **Floating Naval Museum** on board the escort vessel "Maillé-Brézé" anchored on the Quai de la Fosse, and the **Printing Museum** in the main library, which gave rise to the **Media Library** at 15 Rue de l'Héronnière.

The media library.

The **Planetarium** on Square Moisan is a huge celestial vault 26 ft. in diameter, one of the finest of its kind in France.

Among the modern architectural designs, the most spectacular is without any doubt the **Brittany Tower** to which the locals are beginning to become accustomed. There is also the **"Radiant City"** in Rézé designed by Le Corbusier, the elegant and austere **Regional Palace** upstream from Ile Beaulieu, the harmonious outline of the new **Beaujoire Stadium,** the **"Sillon de Bretagne"** in Saint-Herblain, the **regional hospital,** and the **Congress and Exhibition Centre** in La Beaujoire. Among

the new housing estates, **Ile Beaulieu** merits its name (literally "place of beauty') even more than before because of its attractive buildings. The regional radio station and local TV channel (FR3-Pays de Loire) were the first authorities to take up residence here. The island is linked to the main town by two new bridges with long arches.

Many famous people were born in Nantes, or lived there for some time. Among them were the great politicians Aristide Briand (1862-1932) and Pierre Waldeck-Rousseau (1846-1904), General Pierre Cambronne (1770-1842), the author Jules Verne (1828-

1885), journalists Jean-Gabriel Peltier (1765-1825) and Morvan-Lebesque (1911-1970), the writer and journalist Jules Vallès (1832-1885), the surrealist Benjamin Péret (1899-1959), the musician Paul Ladmirault (1877-1944), and the essayist and poet Michel Manoll (1911-1984). I have listed many, many more in my book entitled **"Nantes"** and my only regret is my failure to mention the vigourous talents of the novelist Henri Dumoulin.

Nestling amidst the neighbouring woodland, fields, and gardens, the nearby villages of the 19th century have all become towns. One such is Rezé on the banks of the

Cours des 50-Otages.

Loire, a town with a very ancient history since it even rivalled Nantes until the 6th century when it was known as **Ratiatum Pictone.** It was in Rezé that Crassus, one of Caesar's lieutenants, ordered the mass production of the low, light, swift galleys used by the Romans to defeat the Veneti whose heavy, high-sided vessels took much longer to manoeuvre.

The **Trentemoult District** in Rezé was well-known in the 18th century for its fishermen, who had a reputation for being the bravest

The Brittany Tower.

The Regional Offices to the east of Beaulieu.

and cleverest in the region. They had no hesitation in setting their flat-bottomed boats on course for the high seas, venturing as far as Lorient in one direction and La Rochelle or even Bordeaux in the other. Each barge had a three-man crew and was absent from port for ten or more days. At the end of September, they fished herring in the Baie de Mesquer.

There have been similar population explosions in the other ancient villages such as **Saint-Herblain, Carquefou,** and **Saint-Sébastien-sur-Loire.** In the 1820's **Orvault** (literally Valley of Gold), a town which now has a population of approximately 25,000, was a tiny village with only one hundred inhabitants, set in the midst of a dense chestnut forest that was the haunt of wolves, foxes and wild boar. The writer Edouard Richer stayed here for some time. "On Whitmonday," he wrote, "youths and young girls in search of domestic employment, all carrying a large bouquet, would gather in the graveyard where the farmers would come and engage their servants. The day ended in games and dancing".

Since then, everything has changed, undergone a total transformation. Greater Nantes now has more than 500,000 inhabitants.

The "Maillé-Brézé",
a floating museum
anchored alongside
the Quai de la Fosse. ▶

R.Erdre.

The keep in Oudon. ▶

NORT-SUR-ERDRE

19 miles N of Nantes

With a current population of approximately 5,000, this old town set amidst trees and pastures, and once the site of a large number of watermills, is now one of the most pleasant meeting places of the riding fraternity, for it has a training centre and a **race track.** A recently-constructed 10-hectare **lake** on the R.Erdre in the town centre provides all the enjoyment of water sports.

The church is worth a visit for, among other things, its beautiful stained glass windows. **St. George's Bridge** has three spans.

The **Château de Port-Mulon,** which is occasionally used as an exhibition centre, stands in the midst of a very attractive park with a number of rare trees.

There are many delightful places for a stroll, especially around the hamlets of **La Poupinière** and **Tomblehoux,** and at the **Quiheix Lock** which marks the start of the Nantes-Brest Canal.

OUDON

15 miles NE of Nantes

Among the ruins of a 13th-century fortress stands the 14th-century **keep,** a six-sided tower 105 ft. high. There is a staircase to the top and the view stretches for miles across the magnificent Loire Valley.

A few miles away in the Nantes direction, still on the right bank of the river, is the **Château de Clermont** (17th century), perched on an outcrop of rock. It belonged to the actor Louis de Funès who had it restored.

Not far from **Mauves-sur-Loire** is the 17th-century **Château de la Seilleraye,** built to designs by the famous architect François Mansart. The park was laid out by André Le Nôtre. This fine country house is now a convalescent home.

PAIMBOEUF

28 miles NE of Nantes

Because of its geographical situation at the mouth of the Loire, Paimboeuf enjoyed a period of enormous prosperity when the shipowners from Nantes prepared their vessels, in particular for whaling. The river was becoming increasingly silted up and the large sailing ships were unable to sail any further inland. They would therefore offload their cargoes here, in a harbour that was then **the main outer port of Nantes.**

Of those days, there remain the quays, especially the **Quai Eole** lined with **private mansions** built in the style of the days of the Napoleonic Empire. **St. Louis' Church** surprises visitors because of its Byzantine architecture. It has an attractive dome and a marble altar that came from the old Cistercian abbey in **Buzay** (12th century) of which only one tower has been left standing. It is particularly pleasant to stroll through the **old town,** along the Rue du Faisan and other narrow streets leading to the Rue Pierre-Jubeau. The former harbour is still protected by a stone breakwater built in 1782.

The chemicals industry, oil-refining, and precision engineering have brought some activity back to the town and it will no doubt expand further as the the development of the estuary is gradually completed.

The nave in St. Louis' Church. ▶

The R. Loire from Champtoceaux (previous pages).

90

The small **harbour** of **Le Pe lerin** in the Nantes direction ha specialised in elver fishing. No far away is the **Château d Briord,** with its French-sty dome topped by a bellturret. dates from the 18th century. Als built at that time was the **Châtea d'Aux** overlooking the R.Loire i **La Montagne.** The Republica army used it as a fortress durin the French Revolution. We sha come back to **Saint-Jean-de Boiseau** later on.

The ferry across the lowe reaches of the R.Indre. ▶

Quai Eole.

The Château d'Aux.

A narrow street in Piriac-sur-Mer.

PIRIAC-SUR-MER

9 miles NW of Guérande

It is said that **King Solomon's Tomb** lies beneath the ruins of a town that was once swallowed up by the waves beyond the harbour, offshore from the **Pointe du Castelli.** The tomb and the king's vast fortune. The Little People are said to stand guard over it, and they must do a good job because it has not yet been discovered, while **Almanzor's Tomb** is clearly visible, a large flat stone approximately 16 ft. long full of mysterious cavities and hollows reminiscent of cups.

What with the fairytale town and the tombs with the strange names, it might be appropriate to mention the Phoenicians, for it has been proved that these daring navigators and wily tradesmen owned establishments all along the Iberian and Atlantic coasts. After all, any legend has some grain of truth in it.

Whatever the case here, this area of the coast, the so-called **Wild Coast,** with its strangely-shaped rocks, is the magical domain of the Little People, which means that it has been inhabited for many a long year.

Piriac is known to have existed at least since the 6th century, and its **harbour** was one of the busiest in the locality. Some of the locals even set sail for Newfoundland to catch cod.

A **crypt** is all that remains of a 13th-century chapel above which the present parish church was built in the 18th century. And there are a number of **old houses** (16th and 17th centuries) in the Rue de la Ridondaine and on the Place de Pennerez.

Nearly 4 miles offshore is the island of **Dumet,** once an English possession, now a major bird sanctuary.

The author Alphonse de Châteaubriant owned a house in Piriac.

Piriac-sur-Mer : the harbour. ▶

PLESSÉ

28 miles NW of Nantes

Most of the dolmens and menhirs have a legend attached to them. Three miles out of Plessé on the Guenrouët road is a white quartz menhir nearly 8 ft. tall known as **"Gargantua's pebble"**. It is said to be a stone that the giant once had in his shoe. He threw it far away and it fell on the head of a fishwife. She is said to still be beneath the menhir, with her fish. Why fish? Perhaps the Little People have an answer.

In the Pont Woods near Plessé is a pile of stones said to be all that remains of a dolmen destroyed in earlier times. Many of these monuments were demolished when Brittany was converted to Christianity. The locals will tell you that these particular stones are hunting dogs which were turned to stone because their master had gone hunting on a Sunday. Nobody knows whether the huntsman himself escaped unscathed.

PONTCHÂTEAU

30 miles NW of Nantes

It happened in 1709... At the Court of King Louis XIV, there were said to be Jansenists in Pont-château. Strange goings-on were also reported - the Jansenists were said to be building an artificial mound 97 ft. high. The King ordered all activities to cease except for work directly connected with the mound designed to bear a Crucifixion scene. In 1822, Father Gouray took up the work where it had been left off and completed it.

The site as we see it today is based on a design drawn up by St. Louis-Marie Grignon de Montfort. In addition to the **Crucifixion scene** itself, which dates from 1710, there are a number of buildings and statues hidden in the vast park shaded by trees and thickets - **Adam's Cave, the Bethlehem Grotto, the Holy Tomb, the Agony Cave, the Upper Room, the House of Nazareth, the House of the Visitation, the Temple of Jerusalem, the Stations of the Cross, the steps of the Scala Sancta** etc. And this is a major place of pilgrimage.

The Breton Louis-Marie Grignon de Montfort (1673-1716) was a great popular preacher throughout the rural areas of Western France. He founded the Order of the Daughters of Wisdom and the priestly Company of Mary, or Montfortains.

So here we are with a part of Palestine in an area where, for many years, the cult was much more Celtic than Catholic, celebrating Morgan the Good Fairy rather than Mary.

The harbour in Le Pouliguen.

The calvary in Pontchâteau.

The cartoonist, journalist and art critic Henri Bouyer was born in Pontchâteau in 1907.

LE POULIGUEN
4 miles S of Guérande

The delightful little **port** of Le Pouliguen has succeeded in preserving its own character with its white fishermen's houses. It has its faithful visitors, most of whom meet up on the **beach** to the right of the harbour. A coast road flanked by cliffs and rocks leads to the **Chapel of St. Anne and St. Julian** (16th century) which stands facing the ocean. It contains 15th-century alabaster bas-reliefs.

The **Little People's Cave** lies between the Pointe de Pen-

Château and the village of Batz. You won't be able to see the gnomes, elves or fairies because they stay in their palace, gouged out of the rock. However, in the 19th century, one man knew the secret that opened up this world to human beings. He was called Pierre-Marie Cavalin. He was a saltpan worker by profession but as he did not own a large area of marshland, he was poor even though he had a heart of gold. One evening, when a storm was blowing from the nor'west, a poor old woman knocked at his door and Pierre-Marie, of course, offered her hospitality, cordially inviting her to share his one and only buckwheat pancake. Suddenly, the cottage was filled with a brilliant

yet diffuse magical light and the pauper woman changed into a beautiful young woman wearing clothes fit only for a queen. And queen she was - of the Little People! In gratitude for Pierre-Marie's hospitality, she entrusted him with the secret, but there was a condition attached to it. Then she disappeared. On the following night, the saltpan worker was able to enter the magical city. What a wonderful sight! He saw the Little People laughing and enjoying themselves amidst gold, silver, and precious stones. An unbelievable sight. And they were extremely kind people. They allowed him to carry off as much gold and as many diamonds as he wanted. Pierre-Marie, needless to say,

The town hall in Le Pouliguen (above). A new marina in Le Pouliguen (opposite, top). The Fairy Grotto (opposite, bottom).

quickly set to work. Then, weighed down beneath a huge sack, he left the magical palace and the cave... But what sorrow awaited him! All the treasure immediately melted away, like the morning dew beneath the sun's rays. Dawn had broken and Cavalin had been so overcome with happiness that he had forgotten the one condition - he was not to be caught by the sun. Still, the Queen of the Little People gave him a present of a golden dish which he never sold - for the simple reason that it was a magic dish and was filled with good food three times a day. *The moral of the story is that kindness is of the essence and that, even in the face of misfortune, he who is kind is never totally destitute.* It is also said that, despite the melting glances of the sun, Pierre-Marie Cavalin was able to take away some of the treasure and that he buried it beneath the standing stone near St. Michael's Beach.

The treasure is believed to still be there. But the story may or may not be true.

PORNIC

31 miles W of Nantes

Pornic has been described as the Dinard of the Jade Coast, and it's true that, in the summer months, this is a bustling little town. But let's not forget that it used to be a very busy fishing port. In fact, the **old harbour** is still there and above it, on an outcrop of rock, is the 13th and 14th-century **castle** that once belonged to Gilles de Rais. The castle is flanked by massive machicolated towers. The **Huguenots' Cross** in the park serves as a reminder of the Protestants who settled here in 1562 and stayed until after the revocation of the Edict of Nantes. The delightful **Terrace Promenade** runs along the **Retz Gardens** further down the hill. A series of narrow flights of steps lead to the **church** which, among other items of interest, contains a 15th-century statue of the Virgin Mary carved in the Burgundian style.

The new **yachting marina** lies between the **Plage de la Source** and the other beach, **Noë-Veillard.** To the left of this second beach are the botanic gardens from which there is a panoramic view over the Baie de Bourgneuf and the island of Noirmoutier.

On the outskirts of the town near Préfailles is the **Motte Barrow,** two dolmens with side chambers standing side by side. The first one is approximately 39 ft.

The harbour, a busy place during the summer (opposite).

Pornic and its "promenade".

long; the second 36 ft. Both of them are 20 ft. in width.

During the French Revolution, Pornic took part in the struggles against the Royalist rebels, and suffered some damage as a result. It was near the **Huguenots' Cross** that more than two hundred rebels were buried. At the end of the Second World War, the town lay within the area held by the German forces, the so-called **"Saint-Nazaire Pocket".** It was not liberated until 8th May 1945.

PORNICHET

6 miles W of Saint-Nazaire

"Just a few cottages on the edge of a canal leading to the saltpans..." This was Pornichet in the 1820's. And it was still an apt description until c. 1860 when city-dwellers, in particular Parisians, began to have holiday homes built here. Some 20 years before La Baule, then, Pornichet became the attractive seaside resort we see today.

A stone jetty protects the **harbour** in the old town of Pornichet. The beaches, in particular **Pornichet-les-Pins** and **Bonne-Source,** are ideal for families, and in the distance you can see the **Pierced Rock.**

The historian Pierre de la Condamine was born in Pornichet in 1911.

Sainte-Marguerite, which lies in the Saint-Nazaire direction, has a quiet beach flanked by cliffs. As to the tranquillity of **Saint-Marc-sur-Mer,** it was hilariously upset in 1951 when Jacques Tati came there to film "Mr. Hulot's Holidays".

The new marina in Pornichet.

The dunes and main beach at Saint-Brévin.

SAINT-BRÉVIN-LES-PINS

3 miles S of Saint-Nazaire

On the other side of the Saint-Nazaire Bridge in **Mindin,** you are in the Retz region. And the houses are white, the roof tiles pale orange. This part of the old county is also known as the **Jade Coast.**

Saint-Brévin is justifiably proud of its five miles of fine sandy **beach** stretching to each side of the outcrop of rock known as the **Pointeau,** while the resort itself is partly hidden amidst a delightful pine wood. The **church** (1657) is worth a visit even though much of it is more recent.

The area was inhabited far back in the mists of time, as shown by a **dolmen** some 16 ft. long and by the results of archaeological digs nearby which uncovered Roman bricks, stone coffins, and various items dating from Antiquity. Not far from Saint-Brévin was the village of **Montoise** whose destruction in the 16th century is thought to have been caused by a tidal wave.

Here, too, there are folk memories of **a failure on the part of the giant, Gargantua,** an event that is unusual enough to be worth recounting. Before the present bridge was built, people crossed the estuary on a large modern ferry. But many years ago, this ferry consisted of no more than a raft made of timber, planks, and reeds from the Brière, roughly lashed together. While out for a stroll nearby, Gargantua saw the raft and the poor passengers crowded together on it, soaked to the skin. "Hey ! Peasants," he cried, "Why don't you build a bridge ? It would be much better than that, wouldn't it ?" 'But it's impossible", came the reply. "The land isn't suitable." "That's what you think !" answered the giant, picking up enormous blocks of rock as if they were no more than pebbles. He piled them up on the south bank but they sank into the mud. Whatever Gargantua did, the same thing happened and he finally gave up, breathless. In disgust, he urinated in the sound at Paimboeuf before continuing on his way. Of the pile of rocks, only one still emerges from the ground, between Mindin and la Prinais. It is the menhir known as **Meadow Rock.**

SAINT-ÉTIENNE-DE-MONTLUC

11 miles NW of Nantes

This village of more than 5,000 inhabitants is not only an important pony and horse market but also a tourist centre for those who enjoy visiting manors and country houses. From Saint-Etienne, you can wander at will through an attractive area filled with **old hou-ses,** or take a stroll or a drive along the banks of the Loire.

The **Château de la Haie-Mahéas** has painted decorations on the outside walls. It is a fine building dating from the 18th century.

In **Sautron,** the **Chapel of Our Lady of Assurance** (1464) is a very old place of pilgrimage. The stone statue of the Virgin Mary dates from the 15th century.

In **Orvault** (cf. Nantes), the **Château de la Tour** still has the harmonious lines of the 16th century when it was first built, despite alterations in the early years of this century.

Le Temple-de-Bretagne marks the highest point (alt. 296 ft) along the **Sillon de Bretagne** on the southern edge of the last remains of the Hercynian range. Originally, its peaks were higher than the mountains in the Alps.

The artist Yvon Labarre is a connaisseur of the discreet poetry of the rural houses (given powerful expression in the stone buildings), especially in **Bouée** whose **church** (16th-17th centuries) has a 14th-century statue of the Madonna and Child.

The musician Jacques Lechat was born in **Couëron** in 1921.

A ride along the shores of the ocean.

Fishing on the Atlantic seaboard.

SAINT-GILDAS-DES-BOIS

11 miles S of Redon

It all happened so long ago… In those days (11th century), the place was called **Lampridic.** It changed its name in honour of Gildas, the founder of the Rhuys Monastery and one of Armorica's most popular saints. A Benedictine **abbey** was dedicated to him.

The parish **church** is the former chapel of the abbey. Although it has undergone major alterations and been restored, it still has its 12th-century appearance (in the chancel, nave and north transept crossing) and a number of 13th-century features. Overall, it is a combination of Gothic and Romanesque architecture. The last restoration was carried out between 1950 and 1966. The beautiful modern **stained glass windows** were made by Maurice Rocher. The other monastery buildings were also altered and, in some cases, extended.

In fact, all this part of the Vilaine area is characterised by its spirituality, as shown by the many granite Crosses dotted throughout the countryside.

The **Château de Carheil** (18th century) on the banks of the Isac, which was burnt down in 1944, is unfortunately no more than a pile of ruins.

◀ *The stained glass windows by Maurice Rocher.*

The church in Saint-Gildas. ▶

SAINT-JEAN-DE-BOISEAU

11 miles W of Nantes

In the 15th century, Father Jean Goheau of Geneston had the **parish church** built, as well as another sanctuary, the **Bethlehem Chapel** on the Pellerin road in **La Combe.** This chapel stood next to a menhir known as the **Stone of Folly ;** from beneath it gushed a spring. Now, the place was really called **Bétélian,** which is reminiscent of the place near Vannes known as **Béléan** where Druid rites were performed for many years. And the word *Béléan* probably comes from **Bélen,** the great Gallic sun god. **Bétélian,** then, was given a more Christian meaning, taking the name **Bethléem** (Bethlehem). As for the standing stone and spring, they no longer exist.

The village, though, is still well-known, for a quite different reason - its **Folk Group** which provides such brilliant entertainment on so many festive occasions.

SAINT-LUMINE-DE-COUTAIS

18 miles SW of Nantes

Lying on the southern shores of Lake Grand-Lieu, this village used to observe a strange custom that gave rise to much merrymaking and enjoyment at Whitsuntide. Villagers paraded a wooden horse through the town before placing it in the church, in the pew reserved for the lord of the manor. The unusual feature of the horse was that it was made in such a way as to enable a man to get inside and manoeuvre it. It was known as the **Mallet Horse.** To the skirl of the pipes, an oak tree from a nearby forest was also carried through the village and solemnly planted on the square. After the Whitsun Mass, the **Mallet Horse** left the church, went and stood beside the oak tree, and the celebrants danced round about it, while the population looked on for ordinary people were not allowed to approach to within 10 ft. Then the leader of the celebrants sang a satirical song with 99 verses in it telling all the events (and minor scandals) that had occurred since the previous Whitsun. The festivities ended in laughter (albeit rather forced in some cases) and the **Mallet Horse** was taken away to be looked after by a churchwarden until the following Whitsun. Nobody knows whether the festivities were invented by a man named Mallet, but they combined Druid rites symbolised by the oak tree and Biblical ceremonies as the horse could be seen as a representation of the scapegoat. The festivities may no longer be held but the population of old certainly was not short of ideas when it came to enjoying themselves.

The Redois Beach in Saint-Michel-Chef-Chef.

Pointe Saint-Gildas.

SAINT-MICHEL-CHEF-CHEF

6 miles N of Pornic

Why repeat the word "Chef"? In the Middle Ages, the town was a *"chevecerie"*, a term from Canon Law meaning that it was the site of a priory. And over the years, the word became "Chef-Chef". History aside, this delightful little town with its Renaissance style **church** is a very old community, in a region that was inhabited even further back as has been shown by the remains of the Paleolithic and Bronze Ages. Children, though, probably know the town more for the biscuits that are manufactured here. The **Redois Beach** on the neighbouring coast extends into a small **harbour.**

South of Redois, a wide esplanade runs from one seaside resort into the next - **Le Cormier, Port-Giraud, La Plaine-sur-Mer** and, finally, **Préfailles** behind the **Pointe Saint-Gildas,** a spur of rock with a coastal station at the top and coves like **La Prée** gouged out of its base. There have been many shipwrecks in the waters off the headland, among them the "Saint-Philibert" on 14th June 1931 when 470 passengers lost their lives on their way back from a boat trip to the island of Noirmoutier.

Beyond the headland is **Sainte-Marie,** not far from **Pornic** which we have already mentioned. Further south, another busy family seaside resort is **La Bernerie.** This, then, is the beautiful Jade Coast whose history unfurled its secrets for the writer Emile Boutin.

111

Saint-Nazaire Bridge.

SAINT-NAZAIRE
37 miles W of Nantes

In his novel, "Beatrix", Honoré de Balzac described the landing stage in Saint-Nazaire in the following terms : **"The spot was adorned with viscous rocks, granite reefs, and gigantic stones that provided a natural protection for its old church (...), all of them obstacles that were highly unlikely to encourage enthusiasts".** The author remem-bered what he had seen when tra-velling in 1830. It goes without saying that he would not recognise the bustling city of today (3 subur-ban districts with some 70,000 inhabitants), one of the world's leading centres of shipbuilding.

The "landing stage" was repla-ced by a gigantic **bridge** over two miles long. The metal section alone is 780 yds. in length and the entire construction rests on 258 piles made of special concrete. Over a distance of 180 yds. it is supported by tensile cables 198 ft. above the river at low tide. The roadway is 39 ft. wide. It took 17,000 tonnes of steel, 80,000 cu. meters of concrete, and 140,000 cu. meters of stone bedding to protect the two main pylones against the force of the tides. This beautiful, and useful, piece of architecture does credit to modern technology.

Although Saint-Nazaire is a

modern town with a modern outlook, its origins date back thousands of years. It has been proved to be the Gallo-Roman harbour of **Corbilo,** itself built over a Late Stone Age site of which little remains except the **Dessignac Barrow,** a 14-foot high **menhir** and the **Lichaven** consisting of two standing stones topped by a slab. The name, Corbilo, has also disappeared, and been replaced by that of Nazaire, a Christian martyr who was beheaded in Italy c. 52 A.D.

As far as shipbuilding is concerned, **Saint-Nazaire Basin** is 528 yds. long by 173 yds. wide.

Penhoët Basin stretches over more than half-a-mile, its eastern shore being flanked by the **Chantiers de l'Atlantique,** a shipyard capable of building 500,000 tonne oil tankers. Huge liners like ''**Normandie**'' and ''**France**'' have sailed out of these basins.

Other industries include aeronautics, nuclear furnace manufacturing, and precision engineering.

Because of the destruction caused by the Second World War, Saint-Nazaire is a new town. The Germans had built a large base here for 20 submarines. The base was attacked and damaged by an Anglo-Canadian commando raid

on 27th and 28th March 1942. The bitter fighting also resulted in a high death toll among the civilian population. At the end of the war, the Germans retrenched in the area that became known as the "Saint-Nazaire Pocket" and air raids flattened more than 90 % of the town. The rebuilding was carried out to designs by an architect called Noël Le Maresquier.

Before leaving the town, be sure to visit the **Folk Museum** in the Rue du Bac de Mindin where a guided tour includes the submarine "L'Espadon" which was decommissioned in 1985.

Among the modern writers

The Dissignac barrow.

The Folk Museum and the submarine ''Espadon'' (photo by D. Macel, above).

The war memorial (opposite).

The Chantiers de l'Atlantique (on previous pages).

born in Saint-Nazaire are Fernand Guériff and Jean Lainé, who set most of their books in the area. The writer Louis Oury, who was born in 1933 in Maumusson, once worked in the Chantiers de l'Atlantique.

region, in particular around Noir-moutier which was of interest for its position close to the mouth of the R. Loire. Finally, worn out by the fighting, the monks left the island with the saint's relics. They set off in 836 A.D. and did not end their peregrinations until thirty-nine years later, in Tournus (Saône-et-Loire).

The few stops they made on their journey over the years have left us this superb church (even if it appears uninteresting from the outside) in which the **upper crypt** with ambulatory is a highly un-usual feature. The Vikings burnt the church down in 847 A.D. and the nave was not rebuilt until the 11th century, but the same style of alternating brick and stone was retained.

In 1937, St. Philbert's relics were brought back from Tournus. A return journey some eleven cen-turies long!

Nearby is the **Lake Centre** (Maison du Lac), an interesting museum devoted to ornithology.

A side aisle in the abbey church (opposite).

SAINT-PHILIBERT-DE-GRAND-LIEU

15 miles S of Nantes

This is one of the oldest sanc-tuaries in France, or even Europe - a **Carolingian minster** built of pink and white brick and contain-ing the blue Pyrenean marble cof-fin, weighing 2 tonnes, of St. Phil-bert or Philibert, founder-abbot of the monastery on the island of Noirmoutier.

In the early years of the 9th cen-tury, the monks of St. Philbert's had a priory here. The place was then called **Déas.** But the Jutes landed at various places in the

The nave and ambulatory in Saint-Philibert-de-Grand-Lieu (overleaf).

R. Erdre et Sucé.

SAVENAY

22 miles NW of Nantes

This town (pop. 5,700) was not always as quiet as it is today. It was here that the Royalist rebel forces were wiped out on 23rd December 1793. They had formed the "Great Catholic and Royal Army" and some 60,000 of them had set out from Saint-Florent for the famous "west-north-west trip". By the time they reached Savenay, their numbers had dwindled to a few thousand ; after the disaster here, only a few hundred were left. As the Republican General Westermann said, "Vendée no

longer exists (…) I have just buried it in the marshes and reed-beds of Savenay (…) I have crush-ed children beneath the hooves of my cavalry and have massacred the women (…). I have not a sin-gle prisoner to reproach myself with". In fact, Vendée was not dead. The struggle was to conti-nue but the "Great Army" no lon-ger existed.

Nearby, in **La Chapelle-Launay,** the old **Abbey of Notre-Dame of the White Crown** is undergoing restoration. Most of the buildings date from the 17th century.

SUCÉ-SUR-ERDRE

9 miles N of Nantes

In the Erdre Valley, special mention must be made of this increasingly-popular **holiday resort.** The river widens out here, forming a delightful lake with a **marina.** It is a wonderful place for water sports, and angling of course.

A set of buildings called **La Cour Gaillard** dates from the 16th century. The scenic beauty is further increased and enhanced by numerous **watermills** like Procé or La Gannerie, **windmills,** and old **dovecots,** all of them a delightful place for an outing.

Still to the south of Sucé but further back from the river is the 16th-century **Château de Chavagne** which serves as a reminder of Descartes who stayed here for long periods of time in his youth.

LA TURBALLE
4 miles W of Guérande

This village lies between Piriac and Le Croisic and is first and foremost a major **fishing port.** The best time to visit it is during the fish auction when it is at its busiest. The harbour is protected by three long stone breakwaters.

St. Anne's Church is a recent building and is of interest for its architecture. It draws on both the traditional Breton style and modern art and was designed by an architect from Nantes named Yves Liberge.

From the salt marshes of Mesquer to the north down to the salt marshes of Guérande in the south, this is a peaceful place for a walk. And there is no better way to drink in the atmosphere that is so particular to this part of the Guérande peninsula, as poets are well aware.

The fishing harbour in La Turballe.

A muscadet vineyard (above).
The Château de la Noë de Bel-Air (opposite).
A winecellar in the Château de Cléray (below).

VALLET

15 miles SE of Nantes

This pleasant locality is considered to be the capital of Muscadet Country. Yet the whole of Sèvre-et-Maine has been more or less covered in vineyards for many a long year, long before the name **"Muscadet"** came into being and in the days when the wine was simply known as **"clairet"**. This dry, light, fruity white wine is unequalled when it comes to finding the right accompaniment to oysters and other seafood. A more ordinary wine, **Gros Plant,** has now improved in quality.

In Vallet the **Château de la Noë de Bel Air** stands high above the

The tiny Mouzillon Bridge.

Vertou, the Monks' Causeway. ▶

Grand-Ferry estate. It was demolished during the French Revolution and rebuilt in the Italianate style in 1836. Like an erstwhile François Mauriac, its owner, Count Jean de Malestroit, cares for his vines while thinking about a new novel.

You will also be made very welcome in **La Haye-Fouassière** whose delicious "fouaces" (sort of thick pancakes baked in the oven) were mentioned by Rabelais who **"knew the art and manner of eating and drinking well to appease the mind". Also worth a visit are Mouzillon** and its Gallo-Roman bridge, **Saint-Fiacre-sur-Maine** where there is a Byzantine style church, **Château-Thébaud** and its majes-

tic country house, **La Placelière,** not to mention **Monnière, Le Landreau** etc. And it was in **Le Pallet** that the famous philosopher Pierre Abélard (or Abailard) was born in 1079. He defended conceptualism in the celebrated quarrel between university teachers, but is better known for his eventful love affair with the beautiful Héloïse. From Le Pallet, a drive along the banks of the Sèvre will take you to the **Liveau Dam** near **Gorges.**

After a visit to this area which, in many ways, is reminiscent of Tuscany, it is easy to see why it was so well-liked by the Romans. And by the Dukes of Brittany in their turn.

VERTOU
5 miles SE of Nantes

With more than 16,000 inhabitants, this town has been caught up in the population explosion on the periphery of Nantes. Yet it has managed to preserve its own appearance in the wonderful Sèvre Valley so that, although it is a town, the atmosphere is decidedly rural.

One famous son of the old town was St. Martin de Vertou (not to be confused with the saint of the same name from Tours). He was equally energetic but he nevertheless failed to convert the people of Herbauge (cf. Grand-Lieu Lake).

The initial work on the **Monks' Dyke** was undertaken in Louis

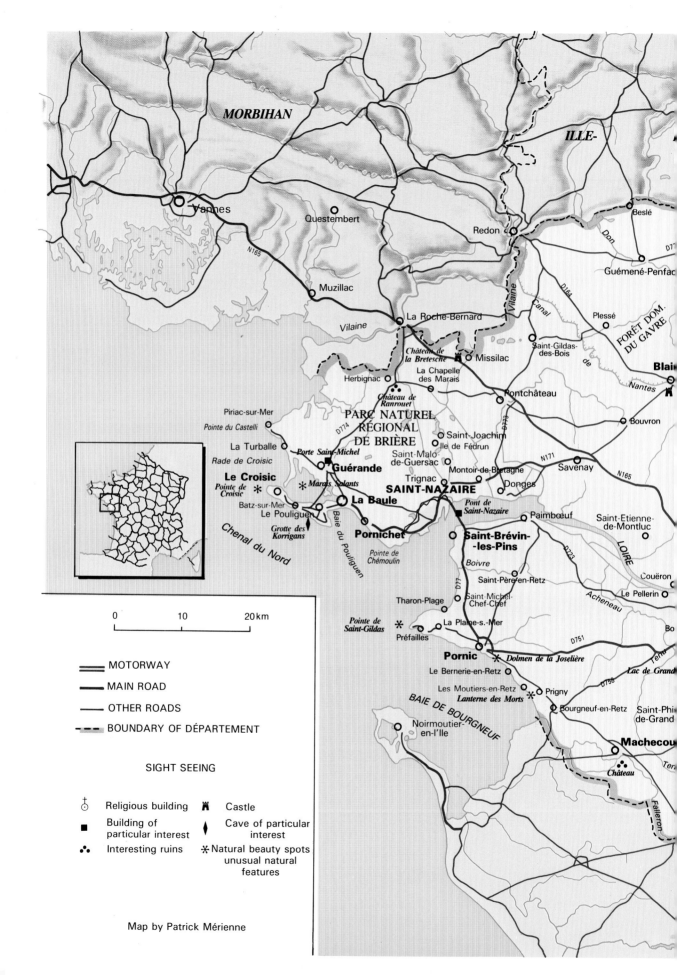

MORBIHAN

ILLE-

Vannes

Questembert

Redon

Beslé

D77

Guémené-Penfao

Muzillac

La Roche-Bernard

Plessé

FORÊT DOM.
DU GAVRE

Vilaine

Château de
la Bretesche

Missilac

Saint-Gildas-
des-Bois

Blai

Herbignac

La Chapelle
des Marais

Pontchâteau

Bouvron

Château de
Ranrouet

PARC NATUREL
RÉGIONAL
DE BRIÈRE

Piriac-sur-Mer

Pointe du Castelli

La Turballe

Rade de Croisic

Porte Saint-Michel

Saint-Joachim

Ile de Fédrun

Guérande

Saint-Malo
-de-Guersac

Montoir-de-Bretagne

Savenay

N171

N165

Le Croisic

Pointe de
Croisic

Marais Salants

SAINT-NAZAIRE

Trignac

Donges

Batz-sur-Mer

Le Pouliguen

La Baule

Pont de
Saint-Nazaire

Paimbœuf

Saint-Etienne-
de-Montluc

Grotte des
Korrigans

Pornichet

Pointe de
Chémoulin

Pornic

Saint-Brévin-
-les-Pins

Boivre

Couëron

Le Pellerin

Saint-Père-en-Retz

Tharon-Plage

Saint-Michel-
Chef-Chef

Bo

Pointe de
Saint-Gildas

La Plaine-s.-Mer

Préfailles

Pornic

Dolmen de la Joselière

Lac de Grand

Le Bernerie-en-Retz

Les Moutiers-en-Retz

Prigny

Lanterne des Morts

Bourgneuf-en-Retz

Saint-Phi
de-Grand

BAIE DE BOURGNEUF

Machecou

Noirmoutier-
en-l'Île

Château

0   10   20km

MOTORWAY

MAIN ROAD

OTHER ROADS

BOUNDARY OF DÉPARTEMENT

SIGHT SEEING

☩ Religious building

🛡 Castle

■ Building of
particular interest

⬥ Cave of particular
interest

⦙ Interesting ruins

✳ Natural beauty spots
unusual natural
features

Map by Patrick Mérienne